foreword

It takes just a handful of ingredients to create a special beverage, but watch how it elevates the ho-hum into an event. A Patio Punch turns an ordinary barbecue into a party, while an after-school Fruit Shake will brighten any youngster's day. Make your regular after-dinner drink a Mint Delight to share with your sweetie and it becomes a memorable evening.

From distinctive coffees to cocktails and coolers, Company's Coming has put together some favourite hot and cold beverage recipes in this convenient book. Our easy, homemade liqueurs are delicious additions to any coffee tray or make wonderful homemade gifts—just pour them into interesting bottles and add fun labels. Whether you want to pamper yourself or celebrate with a host of friends, there's something to cheer about in *Sips*.

Jean Paré

peach lassi

The perfect palate-cleansing drink to serve with spicy curry dishes.

Cans of sliced peaches in juice (14 oz., 398 mL, each)	2	2
Plain yogurt	2 1/2 cups	625 mL
Ice cubes	12	12
Ice water	1 cup	250 mL
Milk	1 cup	250 mL
Granulated sugar	1/4 cup	60 mL
Ground cardamom	1/4 tsp.	1 mL
Ground cinnamon	1/4 tsp.	1 mL

Process all 8 ingredients in 2 batches in blender until smooth. Pour into punch bowl. Stir. Makes about 11 cups (2.75 L). Serves 8.

1 serving: 137 Calories; 1.6 g Total Fat (0.5 g Mono, 0.1 g Poly, 1 g Sat); 6 mg Cholesterol; 26 g Carbohydrate; 1 g Fibre; 6 g Protein; 77 mg Sodium

watermelon cooler

A cool, refreshing beverage with the taste of fresh watermelon and orange liqueur. Be ready with a second batch!

Chopped seedless watermelon (see Tip, page 64)	8 cups	2 L
Orange juice	2 cups	500 mL
Orange liqueur	1 1/4 cups	300 mL
Granulated sugar	1 cup	250 mL

Orange slices, for garnish
Whole fresh strawberries, for garnish

Process first 4 ingredients in 2 batches in blender until smooth.

Garnish individual servings with orange slices and strawberries. Makes about 10 cups (2.5 L). Serves 8.

1 serving: 351 Calories; 0.9 g Total Fat (trace Mono, 0.1 g Poly, trace Sat); 0 mg Cholesterol; 64 g Carbohydrate; 1 g Fibre; 2 g Protein; 7 mg Sodium

orange pineapple cocktail

Bring the tropics to your own deck with this delicious citrus drink.

Orange juice	4 cups	1 L
Pineapple juice	4 cups	1 L
Coconut-flavoured white rum	1 2/3 cups	400 mL
Melon liqueur	2/3 cup	150 mL
Can of pineapple chunks (with juice)	14 oz.	398 mL
Medium orange, thinly sliced	1	1

Ice cubes

Combine first 4 ingredients in large pitcher.

Add pineapple with juice and orange slices. Stir.

Pour over ice cubes in glasses. Makes about 13 cups (3.25 L). Serves 10.

1 serving: 285 Calories; 1.1 g Total Fat (0.1 g Mono, 0.2 g Poly, 0.4 g Sat); 0 mg Cholesterol; 53 g Carbohydrate; 1 g Fibre; 1 g Protein; 6 mg Sodium

patio punch

Place a bowl of skewered maraschino cherries and thin slices of orange beside this hot-weather beverage so guests can dress up their own drinks.

Water	2 cups	500 mL
Can of frozen concentrated orange juice, thawed	12 1/2 oz.	355 mL
Frozen concentrated lemonade, thawed	3/4 cup	175 mL
Grenadine syrup	1/4 cup	60 mL
Club soda	4 cups	1 L
Lemon lime soft drink	4 cups	1 L

Combine first 4 ingredients in large pitcher. Chill, covered, for at least 4 hours until cold.

Just before serving, pour orange juice mixture into punch bowl. Add club soda and lemon lime soft drink. Stir gently. Makes about 12 1/2 cups (3.1 L).

1 cup (250 mL): 141 Calories; 0.1 g Total Fat (trace Mono, trace Poly, trace Sat); 0 mg Cholesterol; 36 g Carbohydrate; trace Fibre; 1 g Protein; 33 mg Sodium

apricot slush

A wedge of lime makes a great garnish and complements the lime juice in this summer sipper.

Apricot nectar	1/2 cup	125 mL
Granulated sugar	3 tbsp.	50 mL
Lime juice	3 tbsp.	50 mL
Ice cubes	10	10

Process all 4 ingredients in blender until frozen slush consistency. Makes about 1 3/4 cups (425 mL). Serves 1.

1 serving: 234 Calories; 0.2 g Total Fat (trace Mono, trace Poly, trace Sat); 0 mg Cholesterol; 61 g Carbohydrate; 1 g Fibre; 1 g Protein; 5 mg Sodium

Apricot Slush

Patio Punch

grape lemonade

The taste of lemon brings a surprising tartness to this thirst-quenching drink. Use interesting containers, such as canning jars, for a fun patio picnic. For those with a sweet tooth, add more sugar.

Water	6 cups	1.5 L
Granulated sugar	2/3 cup	150 mL
Grape juice	4 cups	1 L
Lemon juice	1 1/2 cups	375 mL

Combine water and sugar in large pitcher. Stir until sugar is dissolved.

Add grape juice and lemon juice. Stir. Chill, covered, for at least 4 hours until cold. Makes about 12 cups (3 L). Serves 8.

1 serving: 162 Calories; 0.1 g Total Fat (0 g Mono, trace Poly, trace Sat); 0 mg Cholesterol; 42 g Carbohydrate; trace Fibre; 1 g Protein; 5 mg Sodium

orangeade

Serve this vibrant orange drink over ice in large glasses. You can find citric acid at your local drug store.

Medium unpeeled oranges, cut into 8 wedges each, seeds removed	12	12
Water	12 cups	3 L
Citric acid	3 tbsp.	50 mL
Granulated sugar	3 cups	750 mL

Process orange in blender or food processor until finely chopped. Pour into large bowl or plastic pail.

Add water and citric acid. Stir well. Chill, covered, for at least 6 hours or overnight to blend flavours.

Strain juice through sieve into punch bowl. Add sugar. Stir until dissolved. Makes about 14 cups (3.5 L).

1 cup (250 mL): 228 Calories; 0.4 g Total Fat (trace Mono, trace Poly, trace Sat); 0 mg Cholesterol; 66 g Carbohydrate; 1 g Fibre; 2 g Protein; 3 mg Sodium

rhubarb punch

For a single serving, fill half a glass with the juice mixture and top with ginger ale.

Chopped fresh (or frozen) rhubarb	10 cups	2.5 L
Water	3 cups	750 mL
Granulated sugar	1 cup	250 mL
Orange juice	1 cup	250 mL
Lemon juice	3 tbsp.	50 mL
Ginger ale	5 1/4 cups	1.3 L

Pineapple rings, for garnish
Maraschino cherries, for garnish

Combine rhubarb and water in Dutch oven or large pot. Bring to a boil. Reduce heat to medium-low. Simmer, covered, for about 25 minutes until softened. Strain juice through sieve into large bowl. Allow 30 minutes to drain.

Add sugar to warm juice. Stir until sugar is dissolved.

Add orange juice and lemon juice. Stir. Pour into pitcher. Chill, covered, for at least 4 hours until cold.

Just before serving, pour into punch bowl. Add ginger ale. Stir gently.

Garnish with pineapple rings and cherries. Makes about 10 1/2 cups (2.6 L).

1 cup (250 mL): 140 Calories; 0.1 g Total Fat; (0 g Mono, 0 g Poly, 0 g Sat); 0 mg Cholesterol; 36 g Carbohydrate; 1 g Fibre; 1 g Protein; 11 mg Sodium

ginger cooler

A light, gingery alternative to the traditional root beer float, this summer sipper still needs a long spoon to get the last of the ice cream!

Vanilla ice cream	1 cup	250 mL
Bottles of ginger beer (10 oz., 284 mL, each)	3	3

Divide ice cream between 2 tall glasses.

Slowly pour ginger beer over ice cream. Makes about 3 1/2 cups (875 mL).

1 cup (250 mL): 165 Calories; 4.4 g Total Fat (1.3 g Mono, 0.2 g Poly, 2.7 g Sat); 18 mg Cholesterol; 31 g Carbohydrate; 0 g Fibre; 1 g Protein; 49 mg Sodium

lemon iced tea

Use your favourite tea blends—Earl Grey and Darjeeling are nice variations—for this authentic iced tea.

Boiling water	8 cups	2 L
Granulated sugar	1 cup	250 mL
Orange pekoe tea bags	8	8
Lemon juice	1 cup	250 mL
Ice cubes		
Lemon slices, for garnish		

Pour boiling water into heatproof pitcher. Add sugar. Stir until sugar is dissolved. Add tea bags. Let steep for 10 minutes. Squeeze and discard tea bags.

Add lemon juice. Stir.

Pour over ice in tall glasses.

Garnish with lemon slices. Makes about 9 cups (2.25 L). Serves 9.

1 serving: 100 Calories; 0 g Total Fat (0 g Mono, trace Poly, 0 g Sat); 0 mg Cholesterol 27 g Carbohydrate; trace Fibre; trace Protein; 7 mg Sodium

Ginger Cooler

Lemon Iced Tea

melon and pineapple slush

Pop the honeydew mixture into your freezer up to a day before your event so it has time to become slush. You can add a splash of coconut milk to each glass to give this drink a taste of the tropics.

Chopped honeydew	4 cups	1 L
Pineapple juice	2 1/3 cups	575 mL
Granulated sugar	1/3 cup	75 mL
Ginger ale	3 1/2 cups	875 mL
Melon liqueur (optional)	1/2 cup	125 mL

Honeydew balls, for garnish
Pineapple wedges, for garnish

Process honeydew in blender until smooth. Transfer to large bowl.

Add pineapple juice and sugar. Stir. Freeze, covered, for 12 to 24 hours until frozen but soft enough to remove from bowl and process. Process frozen mixture in blender until coarsely chopped.

Fill 8 tall glasses 2/3 full of slush. Combine ginger ale and liqueur in pitcher. Pour over slush mixture. Makes about 8 cups (2 L).

Garnish with honeydew balls and pineapple wedges. Serves 8.

1 serving: 147 Calories; 0.2 g Total Fat (trace Mono, trace Poly, 0 g Sat); 0 mg Cholesterol; 37 g Carbohydrate; 1 g Fibre; 1 g Protein; 18 mg Sodium

watermelon punch

Chill a tray of martini glasses or wine goblets before serving this pretty drink.

Chopped seedless watermelon (see Tip, page 64)	3 cups	750 mL
Diced seedless watermelon	2 cups	500 mL
Melon liqueur	1/2 cup	125 mL
White rum	1/2 cup	125 mL
Lemon lime soft drink	2 cups	500 mL

Process first amount of watermelon in food processor or blender until smooth. Pour into pitcher.

Add next 3 ingredients. Stir. Chill, covered, for at least 4 hours until cold.

Just before serving, stir soft drink into watermelon mixture. Makes about 6 1/2 cups (1.6 L). Serves 4.

1 serving: 319 Calories; 1 g Total Fat (trace Mono, trace Poly, 0 g Sat); 0 mg Cholesterol; 43 g Carbohydrate; 1 g Fibre; 1 g Protein; 21 mg Sodium

peanut chocolate shake

This is so good and so simple. When someone really needs a lift, chop up a piece of a favourite chocolate bar and sprinkle on top as garnish.

Milk	1/2 cup	125 mL
Vanilla (or chocolate) ice cream	1/2 cup	125 mL
Smooth peanut butter	1 1/2 tbsp.	25 mL
Chocolate syrup	1 tbsp.	15 mL

Process all 4 ingredients in blender until smooth. Makes about 1 1/3 cups (325 mL). Serves 1.

1 serving: 544 Calories; 30.4 g Total Fat (11.3 g Mono, 4.5 g Poly, 13.1 g Sat); 68 mg Cholesterol; 57 g Carbohydrate; 2 g Fibre; 16 g Protein; 326 mg Sodium

peach shake

Use canned pears or apricots instead of peaches as variations for this tasty and healthy yogurt shake.

Can of sliced peaches in juice (with juice)	14 oz.	398 mL
Vanilla yogurt	1 cup	250 mL
Crushed ice (or 4 ice cubes)	1/2 cup	125 mL
Brown sugar, packed	1 tbsp.	15 mL
Lemon juice	2 tsp.	10 mL

Process all 5 ingredients in blender until smooth. Makes about 3 1/2 cups (875 mL).

1 cup (250 mL): 115 Calories; 1.2 g Total Fat (0.3 g Mono, 0.1 Poly, 0.7 g Sat); 5 mg Cholesterol; 23 g Carbohydrate; 1 g Fibre; 5 g Protein; 58 mg Sodium

fruit shake

Bananas and strawberries are a natural combination. Garnish with additional strawberry slices.

Overripe medium bananas, cut up (see Tip, page 64)	2	2
Frozen whole strawberries, cut up	2 cups	500 mL
Milk	2 cups	500 mL
Granulated sugar	2 tbsp.	30 mL

Process all 4 ingredients in blender until smooth. Makes about 4 cups (1 L).

1 cup (250 mL): 156 Calories; 1.7 g Total Fat (0.4 g Mono, 0.1 g Poly, 1.0 g Sat); 5.2 mg Cholesterol; 32 g Carbohydrate; 2 g Fibre; 5 g Protein; 67 mg Sodium

Peach Shake

Fruit Shake

frappé

Pronounced frap-AY, this frosty treat can be made ahead and frozen. Simply thaw and process in a blender when ready to serve.

Cold strong prepared coffee (see Tip, page 64)	1 1/2 cups	375 mL
Vanilla ice cream	1 1/2 cups	375 mL
Crushed ice (or 4 ice cubes)	1/2 cup	125 mL
Chocolate syrup	1/4 cup	60 mL

Process all 4 ingredients in blender until smooth. Makes about 2 1/2 cups (625 mL). Serves 4.

1 serving: 126 Calories; 4.9 g Total Fat (2.9 g Mono, 0.4 g Poly, 6.0 g Sat); 38 mg Cholesterol; 20 g Carbohydrate; 1 g Fibre; 2 g Protein; 93 mg Sodium

coffee punch

The first five ingredients can be prepared ahead of time and refrigerated.
Add frozen yogurt when ready to serve.

Milk	8 cups	2 L
Cold strong prepared coffee (see Tip, page 64)	5 cups	1.25 L
Chocolate ice cream topping	1 cup	250 mL
Granulated sugar	1/2 cup	125 mL
Vanilla extract	2 tsp.	10 mL
Vanilla frozen yogurt (or ice cream)	2 cups	500 mL

Combine first 5 ingredients in punch bowl. Stir until sugar is dissolved.

Add frozen yogurt. Stir gently until combined. Makes about 16 cups (4 L).

1 cup (250 mL): 189 Calories; 5.5 g Total Fat (1.8 g Mono, 0.2 g Poly, 3.3 g Sat); 8 mg Cholesterol; 30 g Carbohydrate; 1 g Fibre; 6 g Protein; 100 mg Sodium

cool coffee nog

Spike this caffeine cooler with mint chocolate sticks. Play with the flavours by using chocolate or coffee ice cream instead of vanilla. Or substitute orange liqueur for the chocolate one.

Cold strong prepared coffee (see Tip, page 64)	4 cups	1 L
Vanilla ice cream, softened	4 cups	1 L
Coffee-flavoured liqueur	1/2 cup	125 mL
Chocolate liqueur	1/4 cup	60 mL

Measure coffee into pitcher. Add remaining 3 ingredients. Stir gently until smooth. Chill until ready to serve. Makes about 6 2/3 cups (1.65 L).

1 cup (250 mL): 272 Calories; 10.8 g Total Fat (3.1 g Mono, 0.4 g Poly, 6.7 g Sat); 38 mg Cholesterol; 30 g Carbohydrate; 0 g Fibre; 3 g Protein; 81 mg Sodium

mocha punch

Combine these layered drinks yourself or place a card with single-serving instructions beside the pitcher of punch so guests can have fun mixing their own. Make sure there's plenty of whipped cream and grated chocolate on hand!

Hot strong prepared coffee (see Tip, page 64)	4 cups	1 L
Granulated sugar	1/2 cup	125 mL
Salt	1/4 tsp.	1 mL
Chocolate ice cream	4 cups	1 L
Cold strong prepared coffee (see Tip, page 64)	4 cups	1 L
Vanilla ice cream	4 cups	1 L
Almond extract	1/4 tsp.	1 mL
Chocolate syrup	3/4 cup	175 mL
Ice cubes		
Whipped cream, for garnish		
Grated chocolate, for garnish		

Combine first 3 ingredients in large bowl. Stir until sugar is dissolved.

Add next 4 ingredients. Stir until ice cream is melted. Makes about 11 cups (2.75 L). Transfer to large pitcher.

Measure about 1 tbsp. (15 mL) chocolate syrup into each of 12 medium glasses. Add ice cubes. Fill with ice cream mixture.

Garnish with whipped cream and grated chocolate. Serves 12.

1 serving: 278 Calories; 10.4 g Total Fat (3 g Mono, 0.4 g Poly, 6.4 g Sat); 36 mg Cholesterol; 46 g Carbohydrate; 0 g Fibre; 4 g Protein; 148 mg Sodium

mexican coffee liqueur

Coffee and vanilla flavours balance the sweetness of this dark, syrupy treat.

Granulated sugar	4 cups	1 L
Boiling water	2 1/4 cups	550 mL
Instant coffee granules	1/4 cup	60 mL
Brandy	2 cups	500 mL
Vanilla beans	2	2

Combine first 3 ingredients in pitcher or large bowl. Stir until sugar is dissolved. Cool.

Add brandy and vanilla beans. Stir. Let stand, covered, at room temperature for about 20 days. Strain through sieve into 8 cup (2 L) liquid measure. Discard solids. Pour into sterile glass jar with tight-fitting lid. Store at room temperature for up to 2 months. Makes about 6 1/4 cups (1.5 L).

1/4 cup (60 mL): 174 Calories; trace Total Fat (0 g Mono, 0 g Poly, 0 g Sat); 0 mg Cholesterol; 34 g Carbohydrate; 0 g Fibre; trace Protein; 2 mg Sodium

almond liqueur

A clear glass bottle really shows off this clear golden liquid with a classic almond flavour.

Granulated sugar	2 cups	500 mL
Water	1 1/2 cups	375 mL
Brandy	2 cups	500 mL
Vodka	2 cups	500 mL
Almond extract	1 1/2 tbsp.	25 mL

Combine sugar and water in large saucepan. Bring to a boil. Boil, uncovered, for 2 minutes. Cool for 30 minutes.

Add remaining 3 ingredients. Stir. Pour into sterile glass jar with tight-fitting lid. Let stand at room temperature for at least 1 week to mature before serving. Store at room temperature for up to 2 months. Makes about 6 cups (1.5 L).

1/4 cup (60 mL): 159 Calories; 0 g Total Fat (0 g Mono, 0 g Poly, 0 g Sat); 0 mg Cholesterol; 18 g Carbohydrate; 0 g Fibre; 0 g Protein; 1 mg Sodium

Kathy

Mexican Coffee Liqueur

Almond Liqueur

plum liqueur

Deep burgundy colour with a nice plum flavour. Serve straight up or with club soda.

Black plums (about 8), chopped	1 1/2 lbs.	680 g
Granulated sugar	3 cups	750 mL
Vodka (or gin)	2 1/4 cups	550 mL

Put plums into sterile glass jar with tight-fitting lid. Pour sugar over top. Do not stir. Pour vodka over top. Do not stir. Let stand at room temperature for 3 months. Strain through fine sieve or double layer of cheesecloth into 8 cup (2 L) liquid measure. Discard solids. Return to same jar. Store at room temperature for up to 2 months. Makes about 5 1/2 cups (1.4 L).

1/4 cup (60 mL): 175 Calories; 0 g Total fat (0 g Mono, 0 g Poly, 0 g Sat);0 mg Cholesterol; 31 g Carbohydrate; 0 g Fibre; trace Protein; 2 mg Sodium

peach liqueur

Good on its own, or as a peach sparkler. Pour the peach liqueur over ice in a tall glass and add twice as much club soda or sparkling water.

Apricot nectar	2 cups	500 mL
Vodka	2 cups	500 mL
Can of frozen concentrated lemonade, thawed	12 1/2 oz.	355 mL
Sweetened peach drink crystals	1 cup	250 mL

Combine all 4 ingredients in sterile glass jar with tight-fitting lid. Store in refrigerator for up to 3 weeks. Makes about 6 cups (1.5 L).

1/4 cup (60 mL): 97 Calories; 0.1 g Total Fat (trace Mono, trace Poly, trace Sat); 0 mg Cholesterol; 13 g Carbohydrate; trace Fibre; trace Protein; 4 mg Sodium

Plum Liqueur

Peach Liqueur

Congratulations
Sherri & Neil

cherry brandy

If you want to give this as a gift, plan to make it several months ahead of time.
To make Cherry Liqueur, use vodka or gin rather than brandy.

Fresh dark cherries (about 6 cups, 1.5 L)	2 lbs.	900 g
Granulated sugar	3 1/2 cups	875 mL
Brandy	3 1/3 cups	825 mL

Poke cherries in several places with skewer or wooden pick.

Layer cherries and sugar in sterile glass jar with tight-fitting lid. Pour brandy over top. Let stand at room temperature for 2 to 3 months, shaking gently once per week. Strain through fine sieve or double layer of cheesecloth into 8 cup (2 L) liquid measure. Discard solids. Return to same jar. Store at room temperature for up to 2 months. Makes about 6 1/2 cups (1.6 L).

1/4 cup (60 mL): 193 Calories; 0.2 g Total Fat (trace Mono, trace Poly, trace Sat); 0 mg Cholesterol; 31 g Carbohydrate; trace Fibre; trace Protein; 1 mg Sodium

tropical rum cocktail

The pineapple and coconut really come through in this rich, frothy cocktail.

Pineapple juice	4 cups	1 L
Whipping cream	1 cup	250 mL
Coconut-flavoured white rum	2/3 cup	150 mL
Dark (navy) rum (or spiced rum)	2/3 cup	150 mL
Lime juice	1/3 cup	75 mL

Ice cubes

Pineapple chunks, for garnish
Lime wedges, for garnish

Process first 5 ingredients in blender until well combined. Makes about 7 cups (1.75 L).

Pour over ice cubes in glasses.

Garnish with pineapple chunks and lime wedges. Serves 6.

1 serving: 352 Calories; 13.6 g Total Fat (4 g Mono, 0.5 g Poly, 8.4 g Sat); 49 mg Cholesterol; 28 g Carbohydrate; trace Fibre; 2 g Protein; 18 mg Sodium

pineapple and lime margaritas

You can salt the rims of the glasses and place them on a pretty tray before guests arrive. Adjust the amount of alcohol to suit your taste.

Lime wedges	2	2
Coarse (or regular) salt	2 tbsp.	30 mL
Pineapple juice	4 cups	1 L
Lime juice	1 cup	250 mL
Gold tequila	2/3 cup	150 mL
Orange liqueur	1/3 cup	75 mL

Ice cubes

Lime wedges, for garnish

Run lime wedges around rims of 6 margarita glasses. Press and twist rims into salt in small saucer.

Combine next 4 ingredients in pitcher. Makes about 6 cups (1.5 L). Divide among prepared glasses.

Add ice cubes.

Garnish with lime wedges. Serves 6.

1 serving: 229 Calories; 0.2 g Total Fat (trace Mono, 0.1 g Poly, trace Sat); 0 mg Cholesterol; 35 g Carbohydrate; trace Fibre; 1 g Protein; 2360 mg Sodium

rush eggnog

Here's a quick and easy way to spruce up store-bought eggnog.

Eggnog	4 cups	1 L
Milk	2 cups	500 mL
Liquor of your choice (such as brandy, Irish whiskey or rum)	1/2 cup	125 mL
Whipping cream	1 cup	250 mL

Combine first 3 ingredients in punch bowl.

Beat whipping cream in medium bowl until soft peaks form. Add to eggnog mixture. Stir gently. Chill until ready to serve. Makes about 7 cups (1.75 L).

1 cup (250 mL): 331 Calories; 18 g Total Fat (5.3 g Mono, 0.7 g Poly, 10.9 g Sat); 114 mg Cholesterol; 25 g Carbohydrate; 0 g Fibre; 9 g Protein; 127 mg Sodium

refreshing cranberry tonic

Float orange slices and whole cranberries in the punch bowl for a nice presentation.

Fresh (or frozen) cranberries, chopped	4 cups	1 L
Water	4 cups	1 L
Granulated sugar	2 cups	500 mL
Orange juice	1 1/2 cups	375 mL
Lemon juice	1/2 cup	125 mL
Tonic water (or club soda or water)	6 cups	1.5 L

Combine first 3 ingredients in large pot or Dutch oven. Bring to a boil. Reduce heat to medium-low. Simmer, uncovered, for about 10 minutes, stirring occasionally, until cranberries are soft. Strain juice through fine sieve or double layer of cheesecloth into large bowl. Discard cranberries.

Add orange juice and lemon juice. Stir. Chill, covered, for at least 4 hours until cold.

Just before serving, pour into punch bowl. Add tonic water. Stir gently. Makes about 13 1/2 cups (3.4 L).

1 cup (250 mL): 193 Calories; 0.1 g Total Fat (0 g Mono, 0 g Poly, 0 g Sat); 0 mg Cholesterol; 50 g Carbohydrate; trace Fibre; trace Protein; 6 mg Sodium

Rush Eggnog

Refreshing Cranberry Tonic

traditional eggnog

Rich and creamy, this classic holiday drink uses raw eggs. Please note our raw egg tip on page 64. Just before serving, whisk lightly to fluff.

Egg whites (large), see Tip, page 64	12	12
Granulated sugar	1 cup	250 mL
Egg yolks (large), see Tip, page 64	12	12
Salt	1/2 tsp.	2 mL
Whipping cream	3 cups	750 mL
Granulated sugar	2 tbsp.	30 mL
Vanilla extract	1 tbsp.	15 mL
Milk	7 cups	1.75 L
Amber (golden) rum	2 cups	500 mL
Whisky	1 cup	250 mL

Ground nutmeg, sprinkle

Beat egg whites in large bowl until frothy. Add first amount of sugar, 1/4 cup (60 mL) at a time while beating, until soft peaks form.

Beat egg yolks and salt in separate large bowl until combined. Add egg whites. Beat on low until combined.

Beat whipping cream in extra-large bowl until just starting to thicken. Add second amount of sugar and vanilla. Beat until soft peaks form. Slowly add egg mixture while beating on low until combined.

Add next 3 ingredients. Beat on low until combined. Chill until ready to serve. Pour into punch bowl.

Sprinkle with nutmeg. Makes about 20 cups (5 L).

1 cup (250 mL): 326 Calories; 16.1 g Total Fat (5 g Mono, 0.8 g Poly, 9.1 g Sat); 177 mg Cholesterol; 18 g Carbohydrate; 0 g Fibre; 8 g Protein; 156 mg Sodium

cranberry perk

No percolator? Set your slow cooker on Low for two hours until the drink is hot.

Apple juice	8 cups	2 L
Cranberry cocktail	8 cups	2 L
Frozen concentrated orange juice, thawed	12 1/2 oz.	355 mL
Granulated sugar	1/2 cup	125 mL
Cinnamon sticks (4 inches, 10 cm, each), broken up	2	2
Whole allspice	2 tsp.	10 mL
Whole cloves	1 tsp.	5 mL

Pour first 3 ingredients into large percolator that has been washed with vinegar and baking soda. Put stem and basket into place.

Place remaining 4 ingredients on 6 inch (15 cm) square of double-layered cheesecloth. Draw up corners and tie with butcher's string. Place in basket. Perk as usual. Makes about 17 1/2 cups (4.4 L).

1 cup (250 mL): 188 Calories; 0.2 g Total Fat (trace Mono, trace Poly, trace Sat); 0 mg Cholesterol; 47 g Carbohydrate; trace Fibre; 1 g Protein; 9 mg Sodium

party punch

Pineapple and lemon lime make a pretty, alcohol-free party drink.

Pineapple juice	6 cups	1.5 L
Water	4 cups	1 L
Granulated sugar	1 cup	250 mL
Envelope of unsweetened lemon lime drink powder	1/4 oz.	6 g
Ginger ale	8 cups	2 L
Ice ring (see Tip, page 64), or ice cubes		

Combine first 4 ingredients in large pitcher. Stir until sugar is dissolved. Chill, covered, for at least 4 hours until cold.

Just before serving, pour into punch bowl. Add ginger ale. Stir gently. Add ice ring. Makes about 18 cups (4.5 L).

1 cup (250 mL): 133 Calories; 0.1 g Total Fat (trace Mono, trace Poly, 0 g Sat); 0 mg Cholesterol 34 g Carbohydrate; trace Fibre; trace Protein; 9 mg Sodium

Party Punch

Cranberry Perk

raspberry mocha

Just the thing to brighten up a cold, gloomy day!

Skim milk powder	1 1/2 cups	375 mL
Granulated sugar	1/2 cup	125 mL
Cocoa, sifted if lumpy	6 tbsp.	100 mL
Powdered coffee whitener	6 tbsp.	100 mL
Sweetened raspberry drink crystals	3 tbsp.	50 mL
Instant coffee granules	5 tsp.	25 mL
Hot water	3 cups	750 mL
Milk	4 1/2 cups	1.1 L

Whipped cream, for garnish
Grated chocolate, for garnish

Combine first 6 ingredients in large saucepan.

Slowly stir in hot water until well combined.

Stir in milk. Heat on medium, stirring occasionally, until very hot and surface is foamy. Makes about 8 cups (2 L).

Garnish individual servings with whipped cream and grated chocolate. Serves 6.

1 serving: 329 Calories; 5.2 g Total Fat (1 g Mono, 0.1 g Poly, 3.8 g Sat); 14 mg Cholesterol; 54 g Carbohydrate; 2 g Fibre; 19 g Protein; 284 mg Sodium

marshmallow coffee

A mellow coffee with a satisfying Irish-cream taste. Perfect as a fireside drink.

Strong prepared coffee (see Tip, page 64)	4 cups	1 L
Irish cream liqueur	1/2 cup	125 mL
Miniature multi-coloured marshmallows	40	40

Miniature multi-coloured marshmallows,
for garnish

Combine first 3 ingredients in medium saucepan. Heat and stir on medium for 5 to 7 minutes until marshmallows are melted. Makes about 4 2/3 cups (1.15 L).

Garnish individual servings with marshmallows. Serves 4.

1 serving: 232 Calories; 5.2 g Total Fat (1.5 g Mono, 0.2 g Poly, 3.2 g Sat); 5 mg Cholesterol; 38 g Carbohydrate; 0 g Fibre; 2 g Protein; 62 mg Sodium

mocha café

You can add a dollop of whipped topping and some grated chocolate to make this extra special.

Milk	1/2 cup	125 mL
Strong prepared coffee (see Tip, page 64)	1/2 cup	125 mL
Chocolate milk powder	1 tbsp.	15 mL

Combine all 3 ingredients in microwave-safe mug. Microwave on high (100%) for about 2 minutes until very hot. Makes about 1 cup (250 mL). Serves 1.

1 serving: 97 Calories; 1.7 g Total Fat (0.5 g Mono, 0.1 g Poly, 1.1 g Sat); 5.2 mg Cholesterol; 17 g Carbohydrate; 0 g Fibre; 5 g Protein; 92 mg Sodium

mint delight

A drop of green food colouring in some whipped topping for garnish gives a hint of the mint flavour to come. Add a chocolate filigree if desired.

Granulated sugar	1/3 cup	75 mL
Milk	1/4 cup	60 mL
Cocoa, sifted if lumpy	3 tbsp.	50 mL
Milk	5 1/2 cups	1.4 L
Chocolate liqueur	3 tbsp.	50 mL
White mint liqueur	3 tbsp.	50 mL

Combine first 3 ingredients in large saucepan. Heat on medium-low, stirring constantly, until cocoa and sugar are dissolved.

Add remaining 3 ingredients. Heat and stir for about 5 minutes until heated through. Makes about 6 cups (1.5 L).

1 cup (250 mL): 211 Calories; 4.1 g Total Fat (1.2 g Mono, 0.2 g Poly, 2.5 g Sat); 11.1 mg Cholesterol; 30 g Carbohydrate; 1 g Fibre; 9 g Protein; 131 mg Sodium

Mocha Café

Mint Delight

mocha mugs

Store a blend of the first six ingredients in a covered container, ready to treat unexpected—or expected—guests.

Granulated sugar	1/2 cup	125 mL
Vanilla extract	1 tsp.	5 mL
Skim milk powder	1 cup	250 mL
Cocoa, sifted if lumpy	1/4 cup	60 mL
Instant coffee granules, crushed	1/4 cup	60 mL
Powdered coffee whitener	2 tbsp.	30 mL

Boiling water
Frozen whipped topping, thawed,
    for garnish
Grated chocolate, for garnish

Combine sugar and vanilla in covered container. Shake well.

Add next 4 ingredients. Stir. Makes about 2 cups (500 mL) dry mix, enough for 10 servings.

For 1 serving: Put 3 tbsp. (50 mL) dry mix into mug. Add 1 cup (250 mL) boiling water. Stir. Garnish with whipped topping and grated chocolate.

1 serving: 103 Calories; 0.7 g Total Fat (0.1 g Mono, trace Poly, 0.6 g Sat); 3 mg Cholesterol; 20 g Carbohydrate; 1 g Fibre; 5 g Protein; 71 mg Sodium

café vienna

*For added flair, dip the rim of a mug into a saucer filled with your favourite liqueur,
then press it into granulated sugar in a separate saucer until coated.*

Milk	1 cup	250 mL
Instant coffee granules	1 1/2 tsp.	7 mL
Ground cinnamon, just a pinch		
Chocolate liqueur	2 tbsp.	30 mL

Combine first 3 ingredients in small heavy saucepan. Heat and stir on medium for
5 to 8 minutes until bubbles form around edge. Remove from heat.

Add liqueur. Stir. Makes about 1 cup (250 mL). Serves 1.

*1 serving: 216 Calories; 7.7 g Total Fat (2.2 g Mono, 0.3 g Poly, 4.8 g Sat); 15 mg Cholesterol;
20 g Carbohydrate; 0 g Fibre; 10 g Protein; 159 mg Sodium*

hot apple cider

A tangy, red punch that looks pretty as is, or garnished with slices of fresh orange.

Cranberry-apple juice	8 cups	2 L
Granulated sugar	1/2 cup	125 mL
Orange slices	4	4
Cinnamon sticks (4 inches, 10 cm, each)	3	3

Combine all 4 ingredients in large saucepan. Heat, uncovered, on medium-low for 15 minutes, stirring occasionally, to blend flavours. Makes about 7 1/2 cups (1.9 L).

1 cup (250 mL): 229 Calories; trace Total Fat (0 g Mono, 0 g Poly, 0 g Sat); 0 mg Cholesterol; 62 g Carbohydrate; trace Fibre; trace Protein; 5 mg Sodium

recipe index

topical tips

Eggs in the raw: When a recipe calls for raw eggs, make sure to use fresh, clean Grade A eggs. Keep chilled and consume the same day it's prepared. Always discard leftovers. Pregnant women, young children or the elderly are not advised to eat anything raw.

Ice ring: Put crushed ice into bottom of 12 cup (3 L) bundt pan. Arrange various fruit pieces in and on top of ice. Freeze for 1 hour. Pour 2 cups (500 mL) punch or fruit juice over top of fruit. (Do not use alcohol in ice ring because alcohol will not freeze.) Freeze for at least 8 hours or overnight. Run warm water over underside of bundt pan. Carefully remove ice ring. Gently place in punch bowl.

Overripe bananas: Too many overripe bananas in the fruit bowl? Peel and cut them into 2 inch (5 cm) pieces. Arrange in a single layer on an ungreased baking sheet with sides. Freeze until firm. Store in resealable freezer bag. Substitute 4 pieces for 1 medium banana. Overripe bananas provide a rich flavour to beverages.

Strong coffee: Use espresso coffee for an extra-strong flavour.

Watermelon flavour all year: At the peak of melon season, chop watermelon into bite-sized pieces. Freeze in single layer on ungreased baking sheet with sides. Store in resealable freezer bags for up to 12 months. Use in a variety of beverages. Enjoy a taste of summer in the middle of winter!

Nutrition Information Guidelines

Each recipe is analyzed using the Canadian Nutrient File from Health Canada, which is based on the United States Department of Agriculture (USDA) Nutrient Database.

- If more than one ingredient is listed (such as "butter or hard margarine"), or if a range is given (1 – 2 tsp., 5 – 10 mL), only the first ingredient or first amount is analyzed.

- For meat, poultry and fish, the serving size per person is based on the recommended 4 oz. (113 g) uncooked weight (without bone), which is 2 – 3 oz. (57 – 85 g) cooked weight (without bone)— approximately the size of a deck of playing cards.

- Milk used is 1% M.F. (milk fat), unless otherwise stated.

- Cooking oil used is canola oil, unless otherwise stated.

- Ingredients indicating "sprinkle," "optional," or "for garnish" are not included in the nutrition information.

- The fat in recipes and combination foods can vary greatly depending on the sources and types of fats used in each specific ingredient. For these reasons, the count of saturated, monounsaturated and polyunsaturated fats may not add up to the total fat content.